Masters of Technic

Level 3

Technic etudes with emphasis on melody

Compiled, edited and arranged by Jeff Schaum and Wesley Schaum

FOREWORD

Numerous concert pianists and teachers were famous for their insights and development of successful piano technic, particularly during the 1800's. This series of books gives students an exposure to the rich variety of this technic heritage along with the benefits.

Level Three presents fifteen different master technic composers. Emphasis is placed on the ***melodic aspect of technic*** for greater student appeal. The exercises are purposely condense·' modified or transposed for this level. Equal hand development is attained by similar exercises alternately emphasizing right hand and left hand. Different key signatures, appropriate to Level Three, give students experience in various hand positions with black keys.

Measure numbers in a small box are included at the beginning of each system of music. This makes it easier to locate measures during the lesson and for written practice assignments.

The exercises are arranged in order of increasing difficulty. While becoming more challenging, the exercises complement the progress in a method book at the same level.

PRACTICE SUGGESTIONS

To derive the most benefit, attention should be given to how the exercises are practiced. ***Careful listening*** is necessary in order to hear a good balance between the accompaniment and the melody. The accompaniment should not be too loud. It is also important to listen for steady and accurate rhythm, and to make sure each finger plays equally loud, especially the 4th and 5th fingers.

Each exercise should be practiced four or five times daily, starting at a slow tempo and gradually increasing the speed as proficiency improves. Several previously learned exercises should be reviewed each week as part of regular practice.

Schaum Publications, Inc.
10235 N. Port Washington Rd. • Mequon, WI 53092
www.schaumpiano.net

I0805707

04-43
KK-1

Composer Index

Wolff - Finger crossings

Adagio ♩ = 69-80

Op. 187, No. 9

Spindler - Imitation study in B-flat major

Allegretto ♩= 108-126 Op. 308, No. 25

Spindler - Imitation study in D major

Allegretto ♩= 108-126 Op. 308, No. 25

Brauer - Left hand etude

Con moto ♩= 100-116

Op. 15, No. 8

Czerny - Left hand stretching

Allegretto ♩= 108-120

Op. 599, No. 40

Spindler - Imitation study in A major

Adagio ♩= 66-80

Op. 308, No. 6

Spindler - Imitation study in E major

Adagio ♩= 66-80

Op. 308, No. 6

Hanon - Velocity study for 4th and 5th fingers

Vivo ♩ = 58-66

Virtuoso Pianist, No. 11

Streabbog - D major scale study

Andantino ♩ = 96-108

Op. 63, No. 1

Concone - Short phrase groups

Andantino ♩= 92-104

Op. 24, No. 16

Gurlitt - Broken chord study

Vivace ♪ = 152-184

Op. 83, No. 15

Krause, A. - Broken octave etude

Adagio ♩. = 69-80

Op. 4, No. 14

Czerny - Broken chord study for right hand

Biehl - Broken thirds

Andantino ♩= 92-104

Op. 139, No.8

Streabbog - Cross hand etude

Adagio ♩= 72-84

Op. 63, No. 6

Cramer - Dotted 8th and 16th notes

60 Selected Studies, No. 25

Adagio ♩ = 63-76

Loeschhorn - A minor etude in 6/8 time

Adagio ♩. = 66-76 Op. 169, No. 1

Cramer - Sustained fifth finger

Sostenuto ♩ = 96-108

50 Pianoforte Studies, No. 2

Biehl - Finger maneuvers

Andante ♩= 84-96 Op. 139, No. 7

Berens - Broken chord etude

Larghetto ♩. = 54-63

Op. 79, No. 3

Burgmüller - 16th note groups

Op. 100, No. 2

Scherzando ♩ = 88-104

Krause, E. - Left hand study in D major

Andante ♩= 84-100

Op. 99, No. 2

Concone - G minor etude

Adagio ♩= 66-80

Op. 37, No. 8

Concone - D major patterns with chromatics

Giocoso ♩= 96-112

Op. 24, No. 7